ALASKA'S WILDERNESS RAILS

From the Taiga to the Tundra

After years of working 16 hours a day, six days a week, senior Engineer Mike Kopcha, left, and senior Conductor Charlie Ingersoll, say they have it "pretty good" these days. Kopcha, from Jersey City, came to Alaska in 1945 on a one-year contract, but stayed for 37 years. He works freight year 'round. Ingersoll decided as a 20-year-old ex-marine that Alaska was as good a place to settle down as any and better than most. He has worked on the line for 35 years, working passenger runs in the summer. **Courtesy: Fran Durner, Anchorage Daily News.**

ALASKA'S WILDERNESS RAILS

From the Taiga to the Tundra

A pictorial review of the ALASKA RAILROAD
by Ken C. Brovald

Pictorial Histories Publishing Company
Missoula, Montana

LIBRARY OF CONGRESS NUMBER 82-80963

ISBN 0-933126-21-2

First Printing   May 1982
Second Printing   August 1982

Typography by Arrow Graphics
Cover Art Work by Bruce Donnelly
Printed by D.W. Friesen & Sons
Altona, Manitoba Canada

Edited by: Michael Aronson, Strazds' Scrivening, Ideamongery. Anchorage, Alaska,
and Jacquelyn McGiffert, Missoula, Montana.

PRINTED IN CANADA

*FRONT COVER: It is said that Alaska is a state of mind. It can also be said that it is a state of contrasts.
Alaska is not all ice, snow and glaciers. In this scene, taken in the summer of 1981, two color-matched FP7's
roll the Denali Express through the beauty of the wilderness on its daily run into the interior.*

PICTORIAL HISTORIES PUBLISHING COMPANY
713 South Third West
Missoula, Montana 59801

TABLE OF CONTENTS

DEDICATION

This book is affectionately dedicated to my wife, whose
tireless patience and understanding made it possible to
construct and complete this book.

ACKNOWLEDGEMENTS

Many individuals have assisted in preparing this book. I want to express my appreciation to the following
people of the Alaska Railroad for their contribution:

Mr. Frank H. Jones, General Manager, who wrote the foreword, and who offered encouragement and the
use of his office and staff for information.

Mr. William F. Coghill, Planning Officer, for his photos and invaluable statistical roster.

Mr. Robert H. Wright, Chief Mechanical Officer, for the locomotive and equipment roster.

Mr. John T. Gray II, Manager, Marketing and Sales, for traffic highlights.

Mr. John Copeland, Traffic Department, for his photo contribution.

My thanks go also to Ms. Fran Durner and Mr. Jim Lavrakas, *Anchorage Daily News*, for their photos. And
to the professional railroaders, whose photos appear in this work—special thanks. They work to make the
railroad work: They helped me find the trains and the men and women who ran them. Without their
generosity and guidance, this work would have been more difficult.

PHOTOS

All photos by the author unless otherwise noted.

Maps, track profile, station list and logo, all courtesy of the Alaska Railroad.

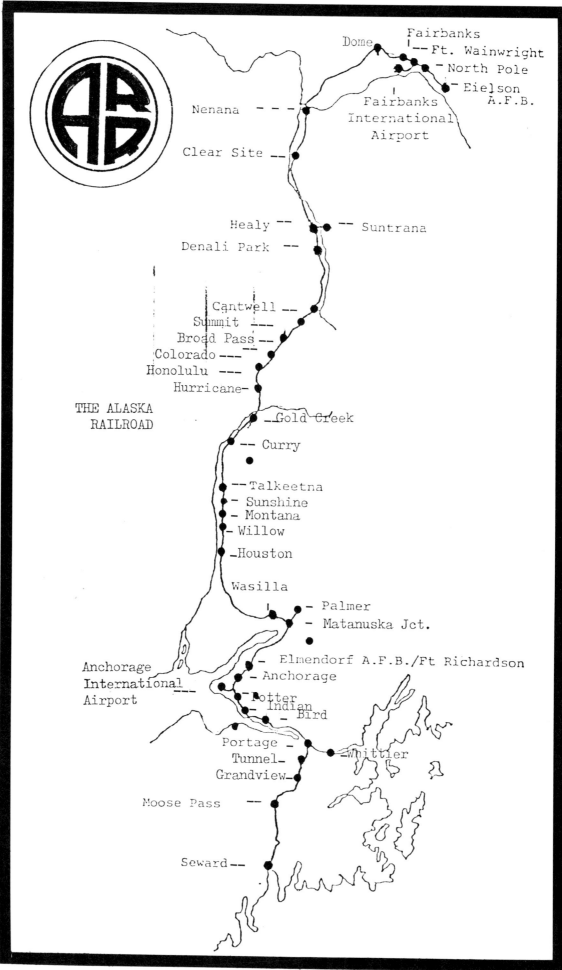

THE ALASKA RAILROAD

THE
ALASKA
RAILROAD

STATIONS	Mile-Post
ANCHORAGE	114.3
— 5.0 —	
CAMPBELL	109.3
— 3.1 —	
TURNAGAIN	106.2
— 5.6 —	
POTTER	100.6
— 7.1 —	
RAINBOW	93.5
— 4.8 —	
INDIAN	88.7
— 7.0 —	
BIRD	81.7
— 7.2 —	
GIRDWOOD	74.5
— 4.0 —	
KERN	70.5
— 6.3 —	
PORTAGE	64.2
— 8.4 —	
SPENCER	55.8
— 4.8 —	
TUNNEL	51.0
— 6.1 —	
GRANDVIEW	44.9
— 4.9 —	
HUNTER	40.0
— 6.2 —	
JOHNSON	33.8
— 4.5 —	
MOOSE PASS	29.3
— 4.8 —	
CROWN POINT	24.5
— 1.2 —	
LAWING	23.3
— 4.9 —	
PRIMROSE	18.4
— 6.4 —	
DIVIDE	12.0
— 5.1 —	
WOODROW	6.9
— 6.9 —	
SEWARD	0.0
(114.3)	

TIMETABLE 110 STATIONS	Milepost
Healy	358.7
—2.4—	
Garner	355.7
—7.8—	
Denali Park	347.7
—5.2—	
Oliver	342.7
—8.3—	
Carlo	334.4
—7.7—	
Windy	326.7
—7.2—	
Cantwell	319.5
—7.0—	
Summit	312.5
—8.2—	
Broad Pass	304.3
—7.2—	
Colorado	297.1
—8.4—	
Honolulu	288.7
—7.3—	
Hurricane	281.4
—7.6—	
Chulitna	273.8
—5.4—	
Canyon	268.4
—5.2—	
Gold Creek	263.2
—5.5—	
Sherman	257.7
—9.2—	
Curry	248.5
—12.3—	
Chase	236.2
—9.5—	
Talkeetna	226.7
—11.4—	
Sunshine	215.3
—6.0—	
Montana	209.3
—7.0—	
Caswell	202.3
—8.4—	
Kashwitna	193.9
—8.2—	
Willow	185.7
—10.4—	
Houston	175.3
—8.8—	
Pittman	166.5
—6.7—	
Wasilla	159.8
—9.1—	
Matanuska	150.7
—8.9—	
Eklutna	141.8
—5.5—	
Birchwood	136.3
—9.7—	
Eagle River	126.6
—7.5—	
Whitney	119.1
—4.8—	
Anchorage	114.3
(244.4)	

TIMETABLE 110 STATIONS	Mile-Post
Fairbanks	470.3
—7.3—	
Happy	463.0
—6.8—	
Dome	456.2
—5.4—	
Saulich	450.8
—11.3—	
Standard	439.5
—7.9—	
Dunbar	431.6
—11.2—	
Manley	420.4
—5.0—	
North Nenana	415.4
—3.7—	
Nenana	411.7
—10.4—	
Julius	401.3
—8.4—	
Clear Site	392.9
—11.7—	
Browne	381.2
—10.0—	
Ferry	371.2
—8.6—	
Lignite	362.6
—3.9—	
Healy	358.7
(111.6)	

TIMETABLE 110 STATIONS	Mile-Post
Portage	F 12.4
— 5.3 —	
Moraine	F 7.1
— 7.1 —	
Whittier	F 0.0

TIMETABLE 110 STATIONS	Mile-Post
Palmer	A 6.5
— 6.5 —	
Matanuska	A 0.0

TIME TABLE 110 STATIONS	Mile-Post
Eielson	G 28.0
— 12.1 —	
North.Pole	G 15.9
— 12.1 —	
Ft. Wainwright	G 3.8
— 3.8 —	
Fairbanks	G 0.0

FOREWORD

The state of Alaska has an enormous wealth of natural resources and scenic wonders. But to develop this richness and to provide a view of the geographical marvels, the Alaska Railroad was required to overcome some extremely challenging natural obstacles.

Mountain ranges, ice and snow, glaciers and wide, rolling rivers were all part of the terrain that had to be crossed by railroaders who opened up the last frontier. They took it all in stride, and the dedication and "can do" spirit of today's employees reflect the tradition set by those pioneers.

For years, the railroad was the unglamorous and unheralded backbone of Alaska's transportation system. The construction of the oil pipeline began to change this perspective, and today, with Alaska's developing export market, most notably in coal, the railroad is about to enter a new era and once again assume an important role in moving Alaska's freight.

The future of the state and the railroad is extremely promising. The railroad and its employees will be called upon—and I predict will meet—the challenges of the future to assist the orderly growth and development of this great state, America's last frontier.

This book is testimony to the resourcefulness and ability of the Alaksa Railroad's employees.

Frank H. Jones
General Manager
Alaska Railroad

Anchorage, Alaska.
October 1981

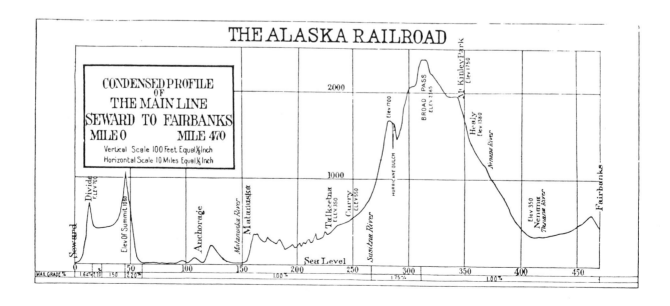

INTRODUCTION

My first look at the Alaska Railroad came in 1975, when the engineering and construction firm that I worked for transferred me to its Anchorage office during the building of the Trans-Alaska Oil Pipeline. The railroad was the key artery supplying the enormous quantities of material needed for that project.

The federally owned Alaska Railroad is a legend even now. It is the railroad which opened the last frontier, earning itself a place in the hearts and lives of all Alaskans and perhaps all Americans. It runs straight north like a giant arrow, passing near Mt. McKinley, the highest mountain on the continent, and crossing the continental divide at 2,363 feet, the lowest crossing of the Rocky Mountain chain in North America.

Adequate surface transportation has always been one of Alaska's foremost needs. Climatic and geographical barriers have restricted land transportation corridors to a narrow trough running through the center of the state, and towering mountain ranges arc along the coast, preventing easy penetration into the interior. These barriers alone have not accounted for the slow growth of Alaska's transportation, however. Alaska's remoteness, its insularity, its provincialism, its tradition of coastal development, plus its sheer size, have all discouraged development of the interior. The only dependable ways to travel, before railroads and airplanes, were by dog sled or snowshoe, horseback or walking. It was difficult to travel by horse because of the scarcity and expense of feed, the immense distances and the boggy muskeg. Traveling on foot, of course, was even more impractical.

When the rails were spiked into place and the first train came rolling over the 470 miles of wilderness roadbed, the game began to change. The meager rail line, carrying small amounts of freight, scratched a sparse income from the inhospitable land until now it has evolved into a modern and well run, although still only marginally profitable business. For decades, it played a rather anemic David in a Goliath state.

The task of the Alaska Railroad was to span a wilderness with a pencil thin line; a formidable and overwhelming task. Nature and economics have not been kind. The earthquakes, the spring floods, the winter snows covering the tracks, and the ice and frost which heave and shove rails out of alignment, all these natural hazards only mimic the business hazards of boom and bust development. And then, perhaps most importantly, as a further deterrent to the railroad's success, suburbia has not yet reached interior Alaska, nor has the region suffered greatly from the effects of industrialization, large scale mining operations, uncontrolled lumbering or many of the other human activities that have permanently scarred other regions of the U.S. No factories or rich farm lands lie along its route. It penetrates a vast frontier that is still not fully opened to human activity. This is a lonely, remote and almost forbidden land.

Tourists flock to Alaska to see a country where time, until recently, has stood still, and where the countryside is still largely unspoiled. No matter where one is, one is only minutes from the wilderness.

Even though by "state side" standards, Alaska's only standard gauge railroad is a short line, it must penetrate a land mass of continental dimensions, an area more than twice the size of Texas.

Since that summer day in 1923 when President Warren G. Harding drove the Golden Spike which formally opened the railroad, its task has been to carry the state out of bondage, and it was the start of an adventure which brought steel rails into interior Alaska. President Harding carried the future of the state in his hands and a promise in his words when he said, "I am glad a generous government understood and carried to completion the construction of the Alaska Railroad. It is not possible to liken a railway to a magician's wand, but the effect to me is the same, for the whole problem of civilization in the development of resources and the awakening of communities lies in transportation.''

This book is not intended to furnish a history of the line nor a review of the state. The subject matter is too large to cover in depth in the limited confines of these pages, and there are others more qualified to write a definitive history of the railroad. In this work we are going to examine the railroad, during the period of 1975–81 in a pictorial review that will convey the feeling of the road and that imprecise balance of machinery, people and the events which turn a nuts-and-bolts mechanical enterprise into something with a life of its own.

Because many readers may be unfamiliar with the Alaska Railroad, I have arranged the material in this book geographically, south to north.

For those who are meeting her for the first time, I am pleased to introduce you.

Those who know the Alaska Railroad will find here an opportunity to renew their acquaintance.

Ken C. Brovald
Anchorage, Alaska.

October 1981

"Into the harsh land they came to harness a land that was cursed with bitter cold, snow and frost. With Engine No. 1, they hauled every cross tie, every spike and rail, every claw bar and nail to a place that was the reverse side of hell.

But Engine No. 1 was there when the Golden Spike was driven at Nenana. There was shouting and there were tears. Engine No. 1 is with us today, enthroned as a fitting monument to the toil and sweat of the bold men whose hardships we must not forget." Author anonymous.

Ex-Isthmus Canal Commission No. 802, brought to Alaska as Alaska Engineering Commission (AEC) No. 6 in 1917. Built by Davenport as a narrow gauge 0-4-0 ST (saddle tank) in October 1907, it was converted to standard gauge about 1930 and used as a shop switcher. Renumbered to No. 1 during 1947, the engine was placed on display at the Alaska Railroad's general office in Anchorage.

CHAPTER 1
RAILS FROM SEWARD — over the Kenais

The Alaska Railroad touches tidewater at three ports—Seward, Whittier, and Anchorage—and operates 470 miles of main line track. Branch lines, sidings, spurs and yard tracks increase the total trackage to 650 miles. These tracks, the most northern in North America, approach to within 120 miles of the Arctic Circle. The right-of-way is but a scratch on the massive face of Alaska.

In the short distance of less than 500 miles, known unofficially as "the railbelt," the railroad connects the frontier. It serves a sparsely settled land where people are sheltered in log cabins nestled throughout the Taiga (Russian for "sharpsticks," referring to the slim, stunted spruce found in both Siberia and Alaska). The line shares its right-of-way with moose, wolves and bear, and little else. It lugs its trains over three mountain ranges, climbs 3 percent grades and tops the Continental Divide at 2,363 feet above sea-level, the lowest crossing of the Rocky Mountain chain, in the very sight of Mt. McKinley, North America's tallest peak, at Summit. The track scoots across 100 miles of flood plains of interior rivers, ending its track at Fairbanks, Alaska's second most populous city with more than 60,000 inhabitants.

As it runs northward 114 miles from Seward to Anchorage, it carries less freight and fewer passengers than it does on the northern portion, but it operates in a difficult terrain, over the mountains and along the shore. Trains grind around 6,004 cumulative degrees of curvature, climb three percent grades to breach two summits, at 700 and 1063 feet above sea level, and squeeze through eight tunnels all the while operating under the threat of snow falls, avalanches and rock slides. But the pattern of freight may change both suddenly and soon because Seward is being considered as the terminal for a coal and grain transfer port. If that happens, the tonnage to be carried may double or triple and the 1702 cars of rolling stock may be doubled to meet the demand.

The problems encountered by the government in building the railroad were tremendous. It hired 5,000 strong, young immigrant men, who were attracted by the 50-cent hourly wage, to wield hand drills, pick axes and shovels. They dumped land fill from horse-drawn carts, pounded a track into place and wrested a right-of-way from the stubborn, inhospitable north country. They struggled, they fought, through and over mountains and rugged terrain, to build into the interior. Constructing the line cost 56 million dollars, more than seven times the amount paid to Russia for the land in 1867.

Supplies had to be moved more than 2,000 miles from points in the lower states. To hold construction costs to $78,000 a mile, the builders spiked down 70-pound rail on untreated ties, with only a "sprinkling of ballast."

The United States got its money's worth from Alaska, purchased at 2¢ an acre. Since 1880, more than $850 million worth of gold, silver, copper, lead and other minerals have been mined. Untold millions of tons of fish, lumber, coal and more recently, the oil discovery, have been harvested from "Seward's folly," proving the wisdom of the purchase.

Once the railroad was built, it was not easy to operate. Wars and depressions, booms and busts affected it more profoundly than those conditions affected stateside rail lines. During World War II, the railroad carried military freight on barely adequate track in a time that saw frantic activity to fortify America's northernmost outpost. Earthquakes and bankruptcy have threatened the railroad equally. General managers for the railroad have fought off successive Secretaries of the Interior, who have urged the abandonment of the line as a disastrous financial failure, claiming that the area between Seward and Fairbanks was not worth developing. But the displaced dust bowl farmers who were resettled in Palmer and the Matanuska Valley during the Depression of the 1930s had reason to be grateful to the railroad. It served as their only lifeline.

The busiest section of the Alaska Railroad is the 62 miles between Anchorage and Whittier. In the summer months it handles numerous auto-ferry shuttle trains each day plus the freight trains which meet the passenger ships and rail car barges. More than 51,000 carloads, for a total of 1.7 million tons, is loaded yearly, and 40 percent is carried through the port of Whittier.

Whittier is the mouth of the railbelt. It came into existence as a result of World War II, because the military was eager to get a second supply route into Alaska. Seward was prey to high tides and high winds, and ships coming up Cook Inlet into Anchorage were vulnerable to enemy attack. There was a great race to blast the two tunnels, 14,140 and 4,095 feet long, through the Kenai Mountains to Whittier. Crews laboring from three faces holed through 18,235 feet of hard rock in a year.

The port has been an immense success since the first rail barge arrived in 1962. It is served by a 12.4-mile cut-off from Portage. Because of heavy traffic, the track and roadbed have been built to main line standards.

The beauty of Alaska is evident in this scene. The Kenai range surrounds Seward. The climb to the summit begins immediately. Grueling 3 percent grades lift the track over the summit. A silver Salmon special waits for passengers on Aug. 16, 1980.

This brief train of Super Varnish consists merely of the General Managers business car "Glacier Pass" and FP7 1510. Seward dock on Jan. 7, 1979. The City of Seward is across the bay nestled against the mountain.

The snow lies deep at Grandview, an ideal playground for the Nordic Ski Club. On March 2, 1980, some 700 skiers took to the high country for a day under blue skies.

Caboose 1080 and Maintenance car G-1019 share the cold night at Tunnel in November 1978. Winter comes early in the Kenai mountains; the long winter darkness has begun.

Charcoal briquet-fired pots are the only effective means of keeping the ice under control in the tunnels. Here a maintenance crew has stoked one set of pots and is preparing to move on to the next. **Courtesy: William F. Coghill, Alaska Railroad.**

A special ski train from Anchorage to Grandview carrying 700 cross-country skiers through the six-tunnel area on the Seward line on April 5, 1977, passes the maintenance sheds at Tunnel. The deep fresh snow is a paradise for the outdoors-minded Alaskans, and the annual ski train to the 1,063-foot high summit is popular with winter sportsmen.

Moose Pass, the rail transfer point to the Kenai Peninsula, is nestled on the shoulder of "L" shaped Kenai Lake, and surrounded by the towering peaks of the Kenai mountains. All is quiet between infrequent trains.

Extra 3002 leads a special train to Seward on Sept. 15, 1979, wrapping its length around a neck of Kenai Lake at Moose Pass.

Ski train to Grandview on March 2, 1980. Charter trains such as this one carry over 13,000 passengers a year.

Looking like a piece of Colorado narrow-gauge, the track threads through six tunnels, reaching for the summit of the Kenai mountains. Two ribbons of steel wind and twist their way up the grade.

The Kenai mountains on the Seward line present a formidable obstacle. The track winds and twists to gain elevation to the 1,063 ft. summit. Here it appears that the track will run directly into the mountain.

A ski train and a Whittier/Anchorage freight exchange tracks at Portage on March 3, 1980. The Ski train has cleared the main, while a brakeman hurries to throw the switch to allow his train to continue on to Anchorage.

Working on the railroad. Two Alaska Railroad workers from Whittier let the sun warm them as they wait for a train to go past their maintenance car. The two were working near Portage on a March day in 1981. Courtesy: Jim Lavrakas, Anchorage Daily News.

The Kenai mountains are spectabular in their mantle of snow. The click of the wheels on the rail joints is barely audible, muffled by the deep snow. But the crews are not deceived by the quiet beauty of the landscape, for they know that at any moment an avalanche can come crashing down, burying their train or stalling its progress. In this scene, steel wheels bite hard on steel rails, taxing the big motors as they grind around Grandview curve, fighting and growling for every foot of grade, as the drag of a 1,500 ton train pulls back with nearly equal force. Courtesy: William F. Coghill, Alaska Railroad.

At Portage, the engine crew sees this view of the passengers loading on July 30, 1978. Autos and other vehicles are loaded first, then the train is backed to load the foot passengers. More than 71,000 passengers and 17,000 vehicles ride the shuttle into Whittier each year. Just a few miles ahead is the first of two tunnels which separate Whittier from rest of Alaska.

GP40 3015 has charge of a tourist special into Whittier on Aug. 24, 1980.

Like a Navy destroyer surging at flank speed through a North Sea swell, GP40 3002 throws up a wake as it charges through a new snow near Portage on a cloudy March 3, 1979.

The shuttle rolls around the mountain into Whittier on Aug. 24, 1980. The thrice daily train provides essential service to the water-locked community. Connections are made at Whittier with ferry ships which provide views of magnificent Columbia Glacier and serve Valdez, a 90-mile water trip.

F7 1504 doubles with GP7 1839 on the shuttle into Whittier on June 5, 1975. Normally, one unit works the short train, but this day the F7 was needed to assist in freight train service from a rail car barge. The 1839 makes two more round trips to Portage before returning to Anchorage late in the day.

-11-

The rules of the transportation game changed with the advent of rail car barges. This picture shows how the **Griffson** *in Whittier in March 1980, made it possible to interchange rail cars from Canadian and U.S. Rail lines.*

A GP30 uses reacher flat cars to pull the freight cars from the yawning mouth of the Trainship **Alaska** *at Whittier on Aug. 21, 1977.*

Piggyback, maintenance-of-way style. The principle of railroading (i.e., you can pull more than you can carry) is demonstrated here at Portage on July 1, 1978. The small track car is dwarfed by the single axle trailer car and load.

FP7s 1512 and 1510 work a special train which carried some 300 Alaska shippers to view the Whittier rail dock facilities on Nov. 17, 1979.

How a railroad went to sea: The Trainship **Alaska** carried 50 freight cars on two decks with a little space for passengers. No autos were carried. The service operated out of Delta, British Columbia (Vancouver) but was not economical and was discontinued late in 1977. On this calm, rare winter day, Feb. 28, 1976, the bright sunshine was in sharp contrast to the usual rain or snow that falls on the Kenai mountains.

From Portage, the Alaska Railroad follows the shore of Turnagain arm, for a distance of some 37 miles to gain a sea level entrance into Anchorage. The track winds around one sweeping curve after another, with the gray salt water on one side and the high fir-studded mountains on the other. Here, on a beautiful day in 1978, the Whittier shuttle makes its daily run to Portage and Whittier with its usual make-up of three cars and a caboose.

Rolling through the quiet community of Girdwood behind GP40 3002, a special train for the Resource Council enroute to Seward is a classic train in its true sense. Color-matched power units and streamlined color-matched cars with a complement of three domes add to the effect. More than 400 holiday frolickers enjoyed the 114-mile trip along the shoreline, past glaciers, over the divide and into colorful Seward on this bright Sept. 15, 1979.

Six axle quintet. Five RSD4s led by 1605 team up to roll a Whittier-to-Anchorage train along Turnagain Arm in September 1975. Twelve of the RSD4s were built in 1953 for the U.S. Army, leased from the Mechanicsburg, Pa. base in 1975, and turned over to the Alaska Railroad in 1978. RSD4s no longer perform road service. Most are stored in serviceable condition or perform work in the yards.

In a mountainous setting, the shuttle rumbles by Girdwood at noon on an October day in 1977. The short train will pick up auto and foot passengers in Portage.

GP30-2501, probably the most used unit on the roster, leads the way near Indian on May 15, 1977, with empty cars for the rail barges at Whittier returning to Prince Rupert or Seattle.

Four GP40s power a Whittier to Anchorage freight along Turnagain Arm on March 21, 1981. The cars had come through the port of Whittier by barge from Seattle where interchange is made with the Union Pacific and Burlington Northern.

Twenty-four cars of a ski special stretch out on one of the few stretches of straight track along Turnagain Arm.

GP7 1839 on the shuttle passes Bird Creek on June 1, 1975, enroute to Anchorage. Only three weeks away from the longest day, it is almost 10 p.m.; the sun is high; and the few passengers can enjoy the beauty of Turnagain Arm.

The longest passenger train in the U.S. It ran in Alaska on Sept. 15, 1979 and consisted of 24 cars for the Alaska Resources Council carrying 700 businessmen to Seward on a promotional campaign.

Three GP40-2s handle a special train along Turnagain Arm on March 2, 1980. The frozen silt and ice from the high tides tear at the road bed, but heavy rock work along the line prevents any serious damage.

Every effort is made by the Railroad to promote tourism. On Aug. 24, 1980, a Glacier Queen special ran to Whittier to allow a day cruise in Prince William Sound. It is shown here a few minutes out of Anchorage scooting through the forested wilderness.

GP7 1808 running on the Whittier shuttle on Aug. 21, 1977, roars by Potter as a track inspector sits safely on the side track waiting for it to pass so he can continue his work.

Leaning hard into the curve off the Potter causeway and separating itself from Alaska Highway No. 1, two GP40s seek an easier grade into Anchorage on Aug. 15, 1979. The road bed was raised above the high water mark after the 1964 Good Friday earthquake and now separates and protects the highway from ripping bore tides which can tear the roadbeds apart.

GP7 1808 kicks up the dust at the Dimond road crossing in south Anchorage on Aug. 6, 1977. The signal on the right is a dragging gear detector.

On a bitter cold February 1976 day, RSD4 1605 crosses Chester Creek bridge in Anchorage enroute to Whittier. The clear blue sky gives no protection from the cold and Anchorage rests in cold white winter splendor.

This section house at Potter, which once sheltered passengers and crews, has been declared eligible for the National Register of Historic Places. The 28-by-36 foot frame structure was built in 1929 and is the only one of four remaining.

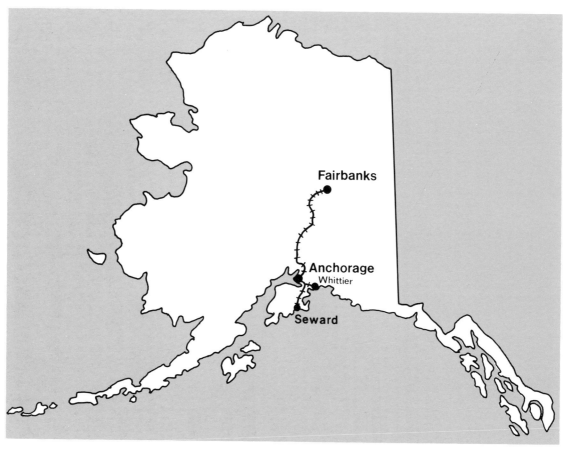

CHAPTER 2
THE HUB OF ALASKA — the Oil and Money Capitol

Anchorage is the hub for the railroad, indeed, the economic center for all of Alaska. Since the discovery of oil in the state and the building of the pipeline, Anchorage has grown to become the oil and financial center of the north. If any company establishes an office in Alaska, most likely it will be placed in Anchorage.

Nestled in the huge bowl of a shoulder of the Chugach Mountains as they sweep into Cook Inlet, the city houses about 200,000 people. Anchorage is still a railroad town. It began as a tent city in 1915, a place chosen by the government to house railroad workers. The site was selected because it was the only place where ships could anchor and unload their construction materials—hence, the name "Anchorage."

Anchorage remains the main operating headquarters for the railroad, as well as the site of its principal yard and repair shops. The general offices are housed in an impressive building in the center of the city. The locomotive and rolling stock service and repair facilities are rated by each general manager as equal to or better than those found on larger railroads. Major work is done on the locomotives in the shops, even to the complete rebuilding of a wrecked unit. Only when a number of units are to be rebuilt are they sent outside to Morrison-Knudsen's facility in Boise, Idaho, or to Illinois Central Gulf's shops in Paducah, Ky.

The diesel era began in June 1944 when it was noted that the use of diesels would eliminate the need to install forced air ventilation in the Whittier tunnels. Two 1000-horsepower Alcos were used to pull trains out of Whittier through the tunnels into Anchorage. The diesels also eliminated the dangerous and frustrating task of watering a steam engine at 50° below zero. The last steam engine ran in revenue service in 1956. The diesel fleet today has 65 units.

The F7s and GP7s were the backbone of the locomotive fleet for many years until the second generation of GP30s and 40s were acquired. Twelve surplus RSD4s were acquired in 1975, but never proved too popular in road service and soon were assigned to local train service and yard service. The Alaska Railroad has long been a hand-me-down child of rail equipment. When the Pentagon planners agreed that a military rail system was not necessary to assure an adequate supply system, 13 EMD MRS1s used throughout the country were declared surplus. All found employment elsewhere. Five found their way to Alaska from the Naval Ammunition Depot at Hawthorne, Cal. Traffic volume fell off about the same time that the Alco-designed EMD powered units arrived on the scene. They were not needed for the purposes intended and are stored as unserviceable.

While the railroad is designed and operated as a 50-mph road, and despite the low density of trains, the track is maintained at a relatively high level. The right-of-way is inspected frequently and repaired quickly. The long winter is hard on the roadbed, with frequent frost-heave damage requiring the maintenance crews to shim the track all winter long, only to remove the shims and trim the track in the spring. Major track work is scheduled each summer. Bridges are continuously being strengthened to handle the heavier loads, increasing their capacity to an E-72 (7200 pounds per track foot) rating.

The Alaska Railroad's trains operate on the single track by train order authority. No block signals mar the right-of-way nor guide the trains. They roll on 115-pound rail, spiked to creosoted ties set in crushed rock/gravel ballast. Communications between the train, offices and individuals is by radio transmitted by microwave. Microwave towers are replacing the familiar land lines which soon will disappear, leaving only the track, a few villages and maintenance sheds. The towers are powered by a new solar energy system. There are no power lines in the country; the throw-away batteries are too labor intensive; land lines are too vulnerable to vandalism. Therefore, the sun-powered system is especially attractive.

From a physical view the line is not much different from other railroads. It is 100 percent diesel powered, using the latest GP40s as well as first generation F7s. The rolling stock pulled by these locomotives is the same that can be found elsewhere. Hi-cube Hydro-cushion-equipped box cars, long piggyback flats, tri-level auto racks can all be seen in the trains.

But into the 470 miles of main line have been squeezed all the operational problems of a railroad ten times its size. The railroad schedules its trains by the tide in order to meet rail barges at Whittier or ships at Seward. The Alaska Railroad fights deep snow along with steep grades and has to protect its roadbed from high water and washouts. Maintenance and operation personnel blast the ice build-up against the bridges, rip rap the banks to prevent mud slides, endure heavy rain, shiver in sub-zero temperatures and live with loneliness and isolation.

The Alaska Railroad did not become part of Amtrak, although they did benefit from the take-over. The Union Pacific sold 12 44-seat chair cars, two diners, four cafe lounges, four dome chair cars (one was destroyed in a train wreck) and six baggage cars, which permitted the retirement of older cars and the streamlining of the "AuRoRa." The beautiful Prussian Blue and Yellow streamliner is a bonanza to the travelers in the state. In 1980, eight coaches from the Southern train, "Crescent," joined the roster, silver cars among the gold, and in 1981, two former Amtrak E-8 six axle passenger locomotives were added. In the short three month tourist season, some 50,000-plus passengers will board these cars. Surprisingly, the Whittier shuttle, with only three cars and running the shortest distance, will carry more than 71,000 passengers in its coach cars and more than 17,000 motor vehicles on its auto-flat cars. The shuttle connects Whittier with the rest of the world and is the only means of getting to and from the isolated community. The shuttle carries passengers and autos through two tunnels to meet ocean-going ships operating to the south coast of Alaska. No sleeping cars ride these rails. All passenger service is operated during daylight hours, although during the long winter, there are more hours of darkness than daylight.

A ride on the streamlined "AuRoRa" or the non-stop "Denali Express" is a lesson in sharing. There are but six scheduled stops along the 356 miles between Anchorage and Fairbanks on the "AuRoRa's" schedule, but the train may stop as many as 20 times to let off or board passengers in the bush section of the route. For many people who live in the bush, the train is the only way in or out, and they plan their life around the train schedule. The train is an experience in human care, a utility and a veritable national resource. The "Denali Express" caters to the tourist trade, and the cultural exchange is a lesson in international relations. Surprisingly, despite sparse population, competing air service and an adequate parallel highway, this train offers reliable and attractive passenger service between the state's two largest cities. It operates on a deficit to provide access to isolated communities along the main line, and it also has proved to be a delight to a growing number of tourists. More and more of them are following the lure of North America's highest mountain and Alaska's greatest attraction—20,320-foot, snow-capped Mt. McKinley, or Denali, The Great One, as it is called locally.

The Palmer branch, just 40 miles north of Anchorage, serving the community of the same name, is beginning to see more activity. It has been almost totally unused for years since the closing of the coal mines on this branch. But today there is a great demand for gravel, and because of an Anchorage ordinance restricting the mining of gravel within the city limits, the ready-mix plants have come to depend upon the Matanuska Valley for their supply. In response to this need, the railroad began to operate two 80-car trains daily, round trip, and more than 800,000 tons of gravel are hauled into the city each year to satisfy the building boom. The round trip is only 100 miles, but it is the most economical way to haul the gravel and a method that is most pleasing to the public. If the same amount were handled by truck, two gravel trucks per minute would share the highway with nervous and frustrated motorists! Intolerable driving conditions are thus avoided, thanks to the railroad.

Although the main track bypasses Palmer and most of the Matanuska Valley farms, some of the farms can be seen from the train during the nine-mile ride from Matanuska Junction to Wasilla. The long, narrow pastures on the prosperous farms seem hemmed in on the far side by a thick forest of hardwood. At milepost 159.8, the thriving community of Wasilla is growing and is pushing its borders to the very limits of useable land. It is a trading center as well as a farming area.

The next 100 miles of track cross a region where streams flowing into the Susitna River once provided some of the best fishing in Alaska. Unfortunately, growing numbers of people along the rail belt brought increased fishing pressure, which quickly depleted the fish population, and the "fishermen's specials" are now but a memory. The trains scoot across the marsh country here and on into the interior for more important appointments.

A strip map of the Alaska Railroad shows a good many dots that, to the outsider, would represent towns. Many are picturesquely named: Birchwood, Kashwitna, Sunshine, Gold Creek, Hurricane, Honolulu, Windy, Lignite, Happy. Most are not towns, however, but section points lived in by maintenance employees, and even some of these have been abandoned. The rail belt is a region of bustling business activity, with major population concentrations at Anchorage and Fairbanks, and minor ones at Seward, Wasilla and Healy. With populations, as sometimes with money, growth feeds on itself. As the rail belt grows, other points in the state decline or fail. Naturally, the Alaska Railroad is the most important economic factor in the development of business enterprise along its right of way.

RAILROAD STATISTICS

No. of diesel locomotives	65
No. of cabooses	27
No. of passenger cars	44
No. of revenue freight cars	1702
No. of freight trains operated in 1980	709
No. of passenger trains operated in 1980	366
No. of employees in 1980	629
Revenue tons carried in 1980 (millions)	1.7
Revenue passengers carried in 1980	150,678
Total revenue in 1980 (millions)	$28.8

1981 Locomotive Roster

Locomotive Number	Number of Units	Builder	Model	Year Built	
1500	1	EMD	F-7	1952	Note 1
1502-1505	4	EMD	F-7	1952	
1506-1507-1508	3	EMD	F-7	1953	
1510-1512-1514	3	EMD	FP-7	1953	Note 2
1517	1	EMD	F-7	1949	Note 2
1530	1	EMD	F-7	1950	Note 3
1601-1612	12	Alco	RSD4	1953	Note 4
1801-1810	10	EMD	GP-7	1951	Note 5
2501-2502	2	EMD	GP-35	1964	
2503 (3051)	1	EMD	GP40-2	1964	Note 6
2504	1	EMD	GP-30	1963	
3001-3006	6	EMD	GP40-2	1975	
3007-3011	5	EMD	GP40-2	1976	Note 7
3012-3015	4	EMD	GP40-2	1978	
570-574	5	EMD	MRS1	1953	Note 8
7249-7324	2	GE	SW	1942	Note 9
7331-7356	2	GE	SW	1941	Note 9
2401-2402	2	EMD	E8	1956	Note 10
P-6, P-7	2	EMD			Note 11
P-10, P-14, P-17 P-19, P-22, P-24	6				Note 12

Note 1. F7s "A" units are even numbered, "B" units are odd numbered. Units 1500-1502-1517 were repainted in a new color scheme, Prussian blue & yellow.

Note 2. 1510-1512 are in a Bicentennial, red, white & blue color scheme. These units, along with 1517, are equipped with steam generators.

Note 3. 1530 is in the original blue & yellow paint, acquired from the Great Northern Railway in 1969.

Note 4. Leased from U.S. Army, Mechanicsburg, Pa. March 1975, they were turned over to the Alaska Railroad in 1978.

Note 5. 1801-1809, were rebuilt by ICG, Paducah, Ky. in 1976-1977, modified with chop nose, upgraded to 1800 horsepower.

Note 6. 2503, was wrecked in a mud slide near Talkeetna, November 1976. Rebuilt in the Anchorage shops, it was renumbered 3051 and named "John C. Manley," in honor of a former General Manager. A 645 prime mover and alternator increased its horsepower to 3000 and raised its class to GP40-2. Since rebuilding, it was involved in a truck accident and is currently being rebuilt a second time.

Note 7. 3001 was equipped to operate as a slave unit and can only be used as a trailing unit. 3001-3008-3009 are equipped with positive traction control.

Note 8. Acquired from the U.S. Navy Ammunition Depot, Hawthorne, Cal. in 1978, currently stored as unserviceable, No. 570 is being rebuilt with a 567 engine and will be renumbered 1818.

Note 9. Powered by two 150 horsepower Cummins diesel engines, and stored indefinitely, they were last used as switchers in Valdez, Alaska in 1974-1977 during the pipeline construction.

Note 10. 2401 Ex Amtrak 430 and Ex UP 957 is equipped with two 645 series, 16 cylinder engines. 2402 Ex Amtrak 434 and Ex MILW 32A is equipped with one 567C and one 567 engine, with a 645 assembly and a 4625 steam generator.

Note 11. Power cars P-6, P-7, Ex Amtrak E8 "B" units carbodies are each equipped with two steam generators.

Note 12. Power cars P-10 through P-24 are equipped for electric power generation on piggyback service.

CABOOSE ROSTER

Caboose Number	Number of Units	Built or Rebuilt	
1023-1026	4	1946	Maintenance-of-way outfit cars
1039-1043	2	1943	Snow train service
1067-1084	17	1949/1976	Road service
1085-1087	3	1977	Road service, wide vision design
1776	1	1949/1975	Red, white & blue colors

PASSENGER TRAIN ROLLING STOCK ROSTER

Description	Seats	Built/Rebuilt	No. of Cars
Coach	44/52	1950/1954	20
Dome Chair	60	1955	3
Passenger/Baggage	40	1945	2
Diner/lunch	48	1959	5
Recreation/bar	0	1945	3
Baggage	0	1961	5
Power car	0	1943	3
Business car	8	1930/1957	1

FREIGHT CAR ROLLING STOCK ROSTER

Description	No. of Cars
Air dump hoppers	76
Ballast hoppers	81
Box cars, all types	255
Flat cars, all sizes	385
Piggyback flat cars	13
Gondola cars	395
Covered hoppers	21
Open top hoppers	336
Refrigerator	16
Tankcars	82
Tunnel ice breaker	1
Locomotive cranes	12
Outfit cars (Maintenance-of-way)	186
Rotary snow plow	1
Russell blade snow plow	1
Snow spreaders	4

The Alaska Railroad's general offices, located in Anchorage along with a locomotive shop and a fair sized yard. Built in 1942 during the F.D. Roosevelt administration, the building is within walking distance of downtown Anchorage.

Nestled on the edge of Ship Creek flats and only a few feet from ocean-going ships, No. 2, the "Denali Express" takes on passengers in Anchorage on May 23, 1981, at the start of the summer schedule. The Whittier/Seward main line curves to the left.

The business car Glacier Pass was renamed Denali in ceremonies on Sept. 8, 1979, in connection with the renaming of McKinley Park.

Just in from Fairbanks, this train is caught in the glare of floodlights, creating an unusual nocturnal scene at Anchorage on Oct. 8, 1977. As it is cold and getting late, the few passengers do not linger.

A quartet of GP30s leave Anchorage on Oct. 9, 1977 with a train of empty cars, fuel and logs for Seward.

Perhaps the idea of piggyback started with the circus train. At any rate, the movement of trailers on flat cars is big business. Caboose 1086 is one of three wide-version caboose on the roster.

GP30 2501 leaves Anchorage, ducking under the Ship Creek bridge enroute to Whittier on April 7, 1979. Winter has not yet released its grip on Alaska, but the GP30s are used to sharing the right-of-way with snow for six months each year.

Some 300 people rode the Papal Express from Fairbanks and interior towns to Anchorage on Feb. 26, 1981 for the visit of Pope John II. Flag-flying 1500 leaves Anchorage for the return trip to Fairbanks.

An 80-car gravel train rolls through Anchorage on Oct. 3, 1977. Three such train loads a day will be gobbled up by the hungry ready-mix concrete plants.

Although the bitter cold and winter storms would halt other forms of travel, they do not stop the railroad nor the men who operate it. An 1800 GP7 works to make up a train in Anchorage in January 1979.

Pumping iron, Alaska style. An old time handcar left Fairbanks on June 22, 1978 on a 365 mile, three-day run to raise funds for muscular dystrophy. Captain Jerry Maddox coaxes Bill Hutchinson, Dan Mantalto and Greg Woodhouse to the finish line in Anchorage.

GP7 1806 crosses Ship Creek in Anchorage with a switch cut on an April day in 1979. This unit was one of nine GP7s rebuilt by the Illinois Central Gulf shops in Paducah, Ky. in 1976-1977. A chop nose was added and the prime mover upgraded to 1800 horsepower, adding years to its service life.

Curt Rudd works a day yardmaster's job on Sept. 11, 1981. The Anchorage yard is a flat yard, requiring extensive switching. Curt communicates with the yard by radio and uses a pair of binoculars, on the window ledge, to direct the operation.

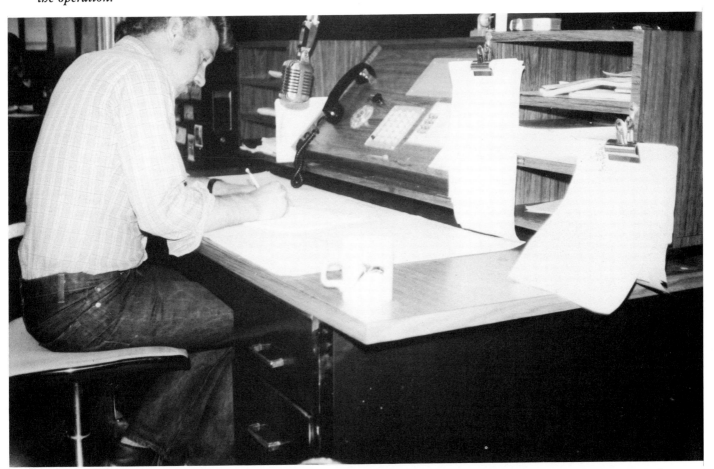

The conductor and enginemen may run the trains, but it is the dispatcher who directs the trains' movements and issues specific instructions to proceed, meet, pass or arrive according to his orders. Ken Greene issues those orders from the Anchorage office, with the tools of his trade at hand: the radio mike, hand telephone, foot pedal radio switch and the train log sheet. On a railroad, it's said, "You can't learn to be a dispatcher, you must be born one."

This general view of the engine terminal, taken in December 1979, includes the material storage yard. Parked on the engine house lead track are five RSD4s. The facilities are the essence of simplicity, consisting of a small pump to fuel the engines and a modest sand tower which furnishes the sand for traction. The profusion of materials needed to keep the railroad operating are stacked neatly for easy access. Courtesy: John C. Copeland, Alaska Railroad.

A caboose is the punctuation mark which concludes every freight train; it is a mobile office; a lookout post. There are about 15,000 caboose in the United States; the Alaska Railroad's 27 have all of the modern conveniences of railroading, including roller bearings, electric lighting, and radiophones.

The sea voyage across the Gulf of Alaska coats the cars with a heavy frosting of ice. "Chippin' Ice" to free the couplers, air hoses and lifting pins is part of railroading in Alaska and is not looked on with envy. This garbage truck on an Alaska Railroad flat car shows the punishment the Gulf can dish out. This scene was taken in the Anchorage yard on Jan. 15, 1980.

If a cosmetic treatment will keep an old "F" running, 1500 should run for many years. Dressed in bright Prussian blue & yellow, she takes the afternoon off to enjoy the Oct. 31, 1980 sun.

Sunday, Aug. 1, 1976 finds RSD4s, F7s, and GP30s laying over in Anchorage. The engine house is tucked in next to Government Hill, the oldest part of the city, dating to early railroad construction days in 1915.

Looking much like an uncompleted second floor, the Anchorage yard office is located so as to allow the yard master to watch the operations from his elevated house.

The track maintenance cars are a familiar symbol of railroading. A stable of Fairmont cars are home in Anchorage for the weekend in August 1976, tucked neatly against a retaining wall.

A diesel-electric locomotive when shut down and on the storage track is very, very quiet, as if it were dead. F7s 1504 and 1505 wait out the winter of 1979 in Anchorage.

Just days before the 1978 tourist season would begin, a display of equipment was out for public view on the tide flats in Anchorage.

Jordan spreader No. 7, called out to do battle with the snow. On Dec. 23, 1978, it is tied up at the Anchorage engine house after working all night to keep the tracks clear and cuts wide.

Just clearing the north yard limits of the Anchorage yard, a three-Geep powered freight accelerates along the banks of the bluffs of Government Hill and the housing section of Elmendorf Air Base on July 23, 1979.

GP7 1802 works the Anchorage piggyback track on Nov. 5, 1978. The road caboose is on, and the power car, which provides electric power to the refrigerated trailers, is on and being serviced. The train will be moved to the running rail; road power will be attached and the cars will be in Fairbanks in time for the business hours the next morning.

You can tell a lot about a company by the way it maintains its equipment. Here, on the rear of a freight train is a brightly painted Prussian blue and yellow modern caboose, reflecting the pride of the employees, with a radio antenna reaching skyward, listening for signals. A fitting punctuation mark. Caboose 1079 is bringing up the rear of an Anchorage/Fairbanks train making an overnight run on May 19, 1979.

1510 is sanded at Anchorage on July 30, 1978, in preparation for another run. The 1953-built FP7 is still doing yeoman work after a quarter century of hard Alaska service.

New Years day 1976 finds FP7 1510 in Bicentennial colors, in observance of the nation's 200th anniversary. The 50-star red, white & blue scheme was designed by Chester J. Mack, Yorba Linda, Calif.

RSD4 1612, assigned to switching chores on Aug. 6, 1977, pushes heavy, three-axle oxygen tank cars toward an industrial plant, leaving its calling card etched into the overcast sky. It is still early in the fall, but the Chugach mountains are covered with "termination dust" the local term for the snow covering the high mountains, signalling the end of summer.

For two decades, most of the trains moved over the road behind General Motors F-unit diesels. These five F7s strike a stately pose on April 18, 1976, ready for the next call to duty. By this date, the aging warriors had reached the end of their service lives and would soon be traded in for newer GP models.

*The Superintendent's "Hi-Rail" car, a '66 Chrysler fitted with flanged wheels, is railed in Anchorage. The heavy springs to support the extra wheels and axles **made a rough** ride on the highway; the railroad route was preferred by those who rode it.*

Railmobiles are provided for key officials for trips over the line, for inspection of the line, and to get to trouble spots quickly. This is one of 15 on the roster, rolling into Anchorage on a June day in 1978.

The lazy afternoon stillness is shattered by the chanting, throbbing roar of 15,000 horsepower urging 5,200 tons into motion at Birchwood on July 22, 1979.

No. 2, "Denali Express" a non-stop to Denali Park, roars through Birchwood, Alaska on July 20, 1981. A classy train on a historical route on the last frontier.

One F7 is all that is needed to move the Transportation Museum to the State Fair grounds in Palmer on Oct. 1, 1977. The eight-car train carrying the historic airplanes and motor buses is shown at Birchwood, Alaska.

The camera moves to the side of the locomotive to bring us close to the mass and muscle of railroading, with a dramatic display of sheet steel, springs, journals, the forceful roar of the 645 series diesels, the high pitched whine of the alternator and the ponderous assemblies that compose a modern "giant of the rails."

On a September 1977 day a northbound freight slips through the Eklutna flats, just north of Anchorage, edges by a rock formation which rivals some of the rock work found in Colorado on the Rio Grande.

Two GP40s hustle a piggyback train near Matanuska Junction on June 7, 1981, the powerful locomotives racing on a good track to guarantee delivery the next morning in Fairbanks.

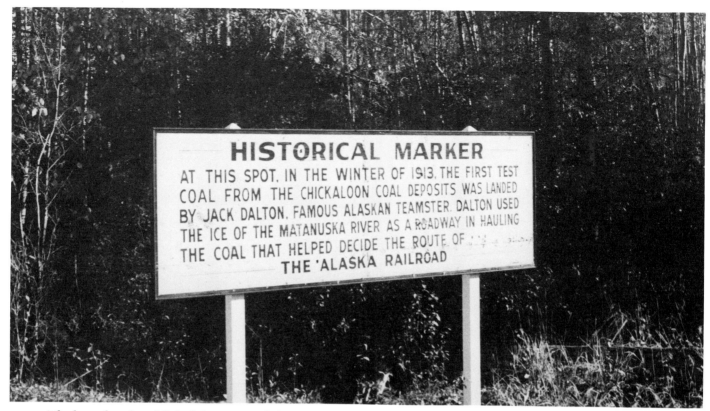

The lure of coal established the route and the need for a railroad at the turn of the century, and coal will sustain it.

The Alaska Railroad is but a tiny scratch on the massive face of Alaska, as this picture shows. A train, looking like a toy amongst full scale mountains, scoots across the Knik River on Sept. 8, 1979. The spectacular Chugach Mountains tower over the placid scene.

F7 1500, assigned to a ballast work train in September 1976, is shown here working its way through what is now Denali Park station. Extensive track work is done in the few short months of summer. Gravel ballast is spread, the track is lined, ties are installed, for winter is hard on tracks in Alaska.

Bicentennial locomotive 1510 is displayed in the Anchorage yard on New Year's day 1976. It was one of the early bicentennial paint schemes applied by the nation's railroads to celebrate America's 200th birthday. The tasteful color scheme, designed by Chester J. Mack, an industrial designer from Yorba Linda, Calif., was one of the better creations. Following the engine's repainting to red, white & blue, with 50 stars, it was put on the daily Anchorage-Fairbanks passenger run. It was kept clean and operated on the point of each run, generating an invaluable amount of good will for the railroad and brightening the countryside.

Men who work on the railroad, make the railroad work. On July 28, 1976, brakeman Doug Simons "bends the iron" in Palmer to allow 3003 to work the yard.

A mixing batch plant is moved into Palmer on July 28, 1978. The city of Palmer sees little train traffic; service is provided on an as-needed basis. The Chugach mountains rise in the background.

The Athabascan village of Eklutna, with a population of 23 natives, is famous for its colorful Russian Orthodox church and its burial grounds. When Russian missionaries founded the community, the natives compromised on their burial practices, and instead of putting the deceased in trees, they built brightly colored "spirit houses." In this scene, No. 6 disturbs the tranquility of the village and shakes the sacred grounds.

GP40 3007 charges past milepost 142 on Sept. 8, 1979, enroute to the State Fair in Palmer. The special is popular with fairgoers, providing relief from hectic traffic.

The camera captured this archetypical Alaska winter scene of a trio of Geeps hustling a Ski train on the Seward line in March 1980.

No. 5, the AuRoRa, waits in the clear at Broad Pass on Sept. 4, 1977 for northbound No. 6. This was the usual meeting place for these trains. Many people would make a Broad Pass turn, from Fairbanks or Anchorage, changing trains here and returning to their home town, a nice one-day trip through Alaska's wilderness.

GP40-2 3003 assisted by a RSD4 leads a freight train through the 14,140-foot Whittier tunnel on Aug. 24, 1981. This is Alaska's back door. All traffic in or out of Whittier goes through the tunnels; there are no roads into the port. A busy day on the Whittier branch may see 12 trains crowding into the small yard to meet passenger ships and rail car barges.

On a November day in 1976, No. 6 loads its passengers at the Anchorage station. The four-car passenger train carries a few revenue freight cars to help ease the winter passenger deficit. The schedule is reduced to two weekly runs during the winter. This train, with regular freight schedules, operates a daily service to Fairbanks.

No. 6 rates 5500 horsepower on its run through Wasilla on April 7, 1979. The extra power is needed to pull the mixed train. Cars and passengers will be in Fairbanks about nightfall.

Civic pride led to a project to paint the Wasilla station Red, White & Blue in recognition of the nation's 200th anniversary, but civic apathy prevented the finish of the job. To prevent an eyesore, the railroad completed it, then subsequently closed the station.

The burgeoning economy demanded a more efficient method of hauling basic construction materials, thus was born the unit train in Alaska. One such train of gravel rolls off the Palmer branch observing the 10 mph speed board.

In May 1978, 2502 leads a three-unit set of GP30s, providing the horsepower to move 80 cars of gravel to Anchorage from the loading tipple at Palmer.

No. 27, the Whittier shuttle, led by GP40 3002, follows the shore line of Turnagain Arm near Indian, Alaska on an October 1976 day. The heavy rip rap protects the roadbed from the ripping bore tides which roar up from Cook Inlet.

In this wild country, the rugged scenery makes the train appear to be a toy. In a picture post card view, No. 5 is caught in the camera lens crossing the Knik river bridge some 35 miles north of Anchorage on a summer day in 1975.

FP7 1514 on train No. 6 scoots through the taiga at Houston. It is a harsh, forbidding land, where civilization is only as wide as the right-of-way. This place has little in common with its Texas namesake.

Where three worlds meet! Snow machines pulling traditional Alaska dog sleds meet Bicentennial colored 1510 in Talkeetna in the winter of 1977. No. 6 heads north into a blustery whiteout.

Wasilla, one of the few stops on the railroad large enough to be called a town. No. 6 stops for a few valley passengers in June 1976. Prominent Pioneer Peak stands guard over the fertile Matanuska valley, permitting the favorable climate and growing season for which the valley is famous.

CHAPTER 3
INTO THE INTERIOR — where the Moose and Grizzlies Play

Because of its vastness and its sparse population, Alaska excites the imagination and encourages thoughts often associated with past frontiers. A trip over the Alaska Railroad provides a lesson in geography and history. Swinging around Matanuska Junction, the train begins a steady climb which will not end for 150 miles, deep in the heart of the interior. Alaska is only now receiving the attention of the world. As the demand for Alaska's resources increases, a new scene may greet passengers who come to visit the open spaces; one day they may view mines and manufacturing plants where now there is wilderness. The influence of developers is already seen in the Mat-Su valley, where huge shopping centers have sprung up in what was the domain of moose and bears only a few short years ago.

As the train picks its way through the marsh country, passing the trading communities of Wasilla, Houston and Willow and crossing Montana Creek into Talkeetna, the tracks are never far from the banks of the wide and meandering Susitna River. Talkeetna is Alaska personified; it's what Hollywood imagines Alaska to look like. The buildings that seem unfinished and the oldtime bars establish the frontier flavor. Life beyond Talkeetna is a life lived between trains. When a train arrives, activity picks up and when it leaves, things slow down again. The fast tempo of living found in the more populated areas is missing here.

At Curry, some 135 miles north of Anchorage, the railroad's attack on the Continental Divide begins with conviction. The one percent grade from Matanuska Junction increases to 1.75 percent. It tests the courage of the crews, strains the traction motors and causes the operating officials to sharpen their pencils to find ways to overcome the high cost of pushing trains over the hill. Additional power is added at Anchorage to provide the tractive capability needed for the 64-mile uphill stretch from Curry to Summit.

Denali Park, the area surrounding Mt. McKinley, is the number one attraction for the railroad, if not for the entire state. The natives call the mountain "Denali, the Great One." Others refer to it affectionately as "Big Mac" for McKinley, until they see it; then they, too, know it as "Denali." The towering 20,320-foot peak is the highest in North America. The park is the next to largest U.S. National Park, second only to Yellowstone, but likely to become the largest if the additional thousands of acres that have been recommended are added to it.

Beyond Denali Park and 244 miles north of Anchorage lies Healy, the site of the largest on-line shipper. In 1980, 8,411 carloads of coal originated here, all of them moving north to the military bases and coal-fired electric generators in Fairbanks. Because new freight crews take over at Healy, the railroad operates a hotel and dining facility here. Trains from Anchorage have been beating their way up a steady one percent or more grade almost the entire distance; their crews are glad to grab a good meal and some rest. The new crews work the short 112-mile distance to Fairbanks and usually make a Fairbanks/Healy/Fairbanks turn.

Coal will be king of freight in Alaska if current negotiations with several Far East consortiums bear fruit. Coal hauling may make the railroad enviably profitable. Considerable study is now going on to choose the location of a port from which a million or more tons of coal per year will be exported. Wherever the port is located, the railroad stands to benefit from the operation.

The 356 miles from Anchorage to Fairbanks is the long-haul route. This line carries two daily passenger trains in each direction from May to September and twice weekly trains in the off season, plus a freight train in each direction. On-line industries provide about 60 percent of the tonnage and about 40 percent of the revenues, mostly in sand, gravel, coal and oil products. Piggyback service began in 1956, using container and trailer vans. This service has grown to a respectable volume of 6,800 trailers yearly.

Nenana lies 297 miles from Anchorage, at the point where the rails cross the Tenana (Ten-a-naw) River and where freight is transferred to river barges. Indian villages on the Tenana and Yukon Rivers are dependent for their yearly supplies upon the summer barges plying the rivers. Prior to the coming of the railroad into the interior, the river villages were served by river steamers operating from the White Pass & Yukon narrow gauge railroad at Whitehorse, Yukon Territory, some 1,000 miles to the east. The Alaska Railroad has provided a much improved service to the Yukon River territory. During the short four-month river season, some 36,000 tons of cargo is transferred to the shallow draft barges and hauled to communities up to 900 miles downriver, almost to the Bering Sea and to Fort Yukon, some 600 miles to the northeast.

Naturally, winter is the most difficult time to operate. In fact, tourists are surprised to learn that the Alaska railroad operates at all in the winter. But although snow and ice may slow the trains, it does not stop them. Actually, the southern end of the railroad lies in the "banana belt," where the moderate midwinter mean temperatures are near 20° F. (The waters of the Japan current off the Gulf of Alaska have a moderating influence on the south coast climate.) But in the interior, at the north end of the line, temperatures can drop to minus 60°, and diesel fuel can solidify and be carved up like a loaf of bread. Snow adds some difficulties, but it causes no problems different from those encountered in the mountains of the lower 48 states. Alaska has somewhat meager precipitation except in the narrow strip along the coast.

Moose, not weather, present the greatest hazard. They hate deep snow and find the plowed out right-of-way an ideal moose path; they feel it is their private domain. The huge 1400-pound animals travel the path between the rails in large numbers during winter. When frightened by an approaching train, they try to escape into the deep snowbanks, then leap back into the path of the locomotive. A dead and mangled moose is the result. Indeed, the railroad has long been called the "Moose Gooser."

If interior winter is a wonder to strangers, interior summer is equally astonishing. Temperatures in Fairbanks, only 120 miles from the Arctic Circle, reach 100°F in the 20-plus hours of daylight. Flowers and berries grow in wild and colorful profusion; they blanket the mountain slopes and canyons, much to the delight of the berry pickers and the bears. Meanwhile, back at the garden, vegetables are growing steadily in the long sunny hours. Cabbages reach a gigantic 80 pounds and are taken for show-'n-tell at the State Fair. Other vegetables also grow to enormous sizes. They are the pride of the Matanuska Valley farmers living just north of Anchorage and are sold in the local stores, with the best placed on public display.

The freight train of today is much different from the train of a few years ago. Box cars no longer dominate, although they still make up a good portion of a train. Today's train is made up of long TTX piggyback flat cars, container flats, automobile racks, "A" frame lumber flat cars, jumbo tanks and jumbo covered hoppers, loaded with feed or fertilizer or flour. Modern 300-horsepower diesel locomotives furnish the power. The "foreign" cars come through the tunnels at Whittier, via rail barge from Prince Rupert, B.C., or Seattle, Wash. The rail car-barges have narrowed the gap between Alaska and other states, closing a 1500-mile rail link to the outside.

Maintaining the track is not easy. Crews working the line in the warmer months are tormented by mosquitoes so vicious and in swarms so thick that they have been known to drive men and beasts wild. In the days of Russian Alaska, prisoners condemned to death were exposed to them to be eaten alive. The mosquito is referred to with deadpan seriousness as the Alaska state bird.

To make matters even worse, the very ground over which the railroad runs often moves. In the Nenana river canyon, the track clings to a wall of soap-like Schist rock. When construction men peeled back the layer of soil blanketing the eight-mile long canyon, centuries-old permafrost began to thaw. The mountains began to creep down the canyon, taking the roadbed with them. Engineers estimate that three million cubic yards of mountain are on the move and so far every attempt to stop it has failed.

Fairbanks sits at the end of the steel. It is the service and supply center for the interior, situated on the huge flood plain between the Alaska range to the south and the Brooks range far to the north. It lies between the river systems that drain more than half the state. These rivers feed the mighty Yukon River, which rises deep in the Yukon Territory of Canada, winds its way through the Yukon and Alaska, picking up tributary rivers along its route, and drains its waters into the Bering Sea. The huge interior remains largely unexplored, unsettled and without roads. Fairbanks quietly serves the Eskimo villages by airplane, river barges, truck and dog sled where there are no roads.

Tourists invade the interior during the short summer season to see the land of the midnight sun and have the experiences of reading a newspaper or watching a baseball game at midnight. In mid-summer, the sun scarcely sets and the weather is warm, but since it is also dry, it can get intolerably hot. Winter in Fairbanks is not only long but extremely cold. The average temperature is minus 12°F. This very low temperature causes moisture to freeze in the air creating an eerie ice fog.

The city dates back to 1902, when a miner found gold nearby. Fairbanks has had its booms, but never busts. The people who work in the northern interior are a special breed, and typical is the tough pioneering spirit in Fairbanks. This area is a haven for the rugged individualist.

If the railroad is fascinating, the state is equally as fascinating. One might say that the giant land mass is bounded, at least theoretically, on the north by the slope oil fields, on the east by Canada, on the west by Russia, and on the south by the U.S. government. It is far from the markets, burned by high costs, eaten, beaten and withered by political hot winds, exploited by capitalists and cozened by politicians. It has been a state of "grab-for-riches," and the early invaders followed the three R's: Rape,

Ruin and Run. This left the state nearly bankrupt. Had it not been for the discovery of oil and the potential of its coal resources, Alaska would have faded into obscurity. It is a state of intense human drama, of humor, of exploitation, of greed and of great adventure. Alaska is bountiful to many and is regarded as an icy frontier, a place for storybook material—romanticized by tourists and exaggerated by sourdoughs. Alaska's economic life is no longer in the embryonic stage; a new era has begun.

Astride the international date line off the west coast is the only spot where, at the same instant, you may look upon two hemispheres, two continents, two nations, two oceans, two islands and two days. It is a land of TOOs and TWOs. Too cold, too hot, too expensive, too remote, and too close to Russia, and home of the tundra, which is too thin to walk on and too thick to swim in. Two seasons: big winter and little winter; two directions: going inside or outside the state; two months of daylight and two months of darkness.

There have been a number of studies and surveys made to determine the feasibility of extending the railroad in other directions, east to Canada, north to the copper and oil fields, west to the coal fields. Surveys have been completed for extensions to the copper field, some 400 miles to the northwest, which would also reach Yukon River points, now served by barges and only for four months of the year.
It may be several years before any of the extensions are economically feasible, but the present line would serve as a core for any such extension. The future of the Alaska Railroad looks bright and encouraging.

The state is on the threshold of securing its place in the economic mainstream along with the lower 48 states. Many new projects are being discussed, including an electric dam near the railbelt, moving the capitol to Willow, some 70 miles north of Anchorage, and the prospects for selling Alaskan coal to Asian countries. In a few years, with a new, vitalized economy and chances for expansion clearer and more certain, the Alaska Railroad may find itself more valuable and profitable. As resources are developed and a market is found for the huge deposits of minerals, it may be private industry and not the state or federal government that pushes the railroad into the wilderness to develop Alaska's remote bush and coast. Have we come full circle and become a country in search of a railroad?

Mountains creep over the roadbed, winds whip snow into 30-foot drifts, moose on the tracks slow the trains, water laps over the track, ice pushes it out of place. With troubles like that around every curve, it is little wonder that railroad workers say, "You catch up in one season, and you get hit by the next."

It is hoped that as civilization spreads its waving arms and throws this vast country into a more modern age, the frontier flavor is not lost and the wilderness rails will continue to be adventuresome, a sturdy asset to the Great Land.

The Alaska Railroad is an exciting railroad, probably the most rugged in the world, but many railroaders still say upon retirement, "It's a good place to spend the rest of a lifetime."

Loela Weimer has the attention of most of the passengers on the Denali Express in the summer of 1981. Some 44 high school juniors and seniors work as hostesses in the railroad's host program. Tourists all ask the same questions: "When will we see McKinley?" "Will we meet bears?" "Where are the moose?" The students' daily contribution to the quality of life aboard the train is considerable. **Courtesy: William F. Coghill, Alaska Railroad.**

Talkeetna station, which serves a thriving community in the Mat-Su Valley. For the railroad it is an important passenger stop, where on a typical summer day more people will board or detrain than live in the town.

The passenger train in Alaska is an experience and an institution. Here, at Talkeetna, back packers and hikers board, giving their destinations by mile post numbers.

On a magnificent Saturday afternoon, May 23, 1981, No. 1, the Denali Express, on its 233-mile nonstop run from Denali Park, roars through Talkeetna. F7 1530 is "pickin' 'em up and layin' 'em down" racing against the schedule.

Two FP7s lead No. 4 across a steel bridge over the Talkeetna River at Talkeetna, setting the deck plates drumming. Here the train enters the backwoods "bush country" where the train is the only means of travel.

On a June day in 1980, a group of "bush" passengers *unload* on a remote section of the line. If there is a single *way that the* railroad comes in direct contact with the lives of the people of Alaska, it is by way of the passenger train.

Snow near the sign post is one of the last remnants of winter in this June 1976 scene. Talkeetna is the "jumping off" place for the adventurous climbers who attempt Mt. McKinley. The climbers take a bush plane to the higher elevations to begin the assault of the mountain.

Part of the fascination of the Alaska Railroad stems from the names of the stations along the line. The Russian heritage remains strong, reflected in the names of the communities on the rail belt ending in "a": Eklutna, Matanuska (Russian for "copper river people"), Wasilla, Kashwitna, Talkeetna, Chulitna, Nenana and Tenana.

Curry, at milepost 248, known earlier as Dead Horse Hill, was once a bustling overnight stop for passenger trains and changing crews. Today it hardly qualifies as a ghost town. With the trend to lengthened divisions, crews no longer change and passenger trains run through, thus costing Curry its only reason for existence. It's easy to guess why it was first called Dead Horse Hill, for here the attack on the continental divide begins with a vengence. The grade steepens to 1.75 percent for 30 miles.

Two fast 40s meet in Talkeetna on May 17, 1980. 3051, rebuilt from wrecked GP35 2503, handles a special train for 400 members of the Resource Development Council who are stopping in Talkeetna for a salmon bake. 3012 on train No. 6 will continue up-country to Denali Park and Fairbanks.

A meeting in the wilderness. The business car "Denali" clears the main line for Extra 3015 south at Carlos, on Aug. 15, 1979. The 356 miles between Anchorage and Fairbanks is almost void of population. The freight carries empty piggyback trailer vans.

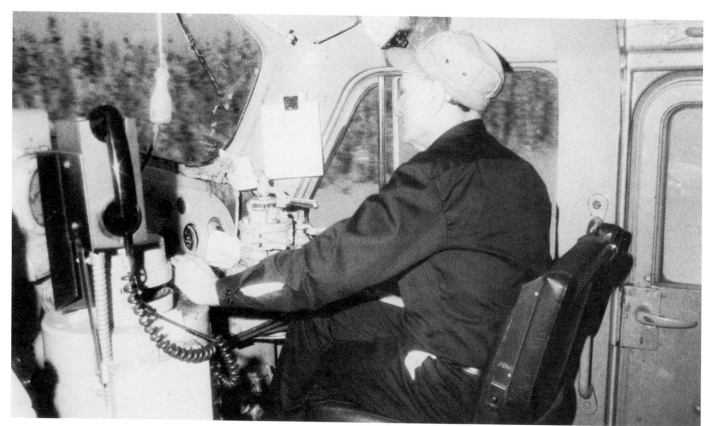

A view from the cab. Engineer Jim Strah will allow no entanglement with moose or auto as he pilots an FP7 through the wilderness on Dec. 23, 1978. His hand is on the throttle and his brake is ready. He can control his locomotive in an instant.

The builders of the railroad early in the century did little cutting or filling. They just followed the contours of the hills. No. 6 dips through a draw and over the ridge into Hurricane on May 27, 1978. A track inspector waits in the clear in his maintenance car while other workers are ready to board for a trip further up the line.

F7 1530 in black & yellow mated with 1510 in Bicentennial red, white and blue works a southbound No. 5, sweeping around a tight curve between Honolulu and Hurricane on May 28, 1978. The dynamics are whining, flanges squealing as the track drops down the 1.75 percent grade into Curry a few miles ahead.

Hurricane is not a regular shop, but local residents are experts at flagging. To quote the lady, "When I see her coming, I grab whatever I can and start waving 'till the engineer blasts me off with his horn." On Sept. 4, 1977 No. 6 stops to pick her up.

There are some tongue twisting names in Alaska, and one wonders who was the humorist that tacked them all over the map. None is quite as ironical as that of Honolulu, Alaska. It is (or was) a small hamlet located 174 miles north of Anchorage, completely void of pineapples, hula dancers or swaying palm trees. It abounds in icicles, snow and a few husky dogs. It is a real pain to the railroad, for it is one of the line's heaviest snow areas, often with six feet of snow. But it provides good publicity. Alaska visitors look for it, and if the train stops, like to have their picture taken by the sign.

Famous one-span Hurricane Bridge at milepost 384.2, traverses a gorge 384 feet wide. There is a drop of 296 feet to the Chulitna river. Trains cross at five mph, and only the most blase passengers are not at the windows to view the crossing. **Courtesy: William Coghill, Alaska Railroad.**

Backgammon is believed to be the first game in which brain power rather than physical strength was tested. The originator is not known, but Cleopatra and Julius Caesar played backgammon (as well as other games) along the banks of the Nile 4,000 years ago. On train No. 6, during the Christmas season of 1978, the author's two sons, Russ & Scott Brovald, test their skill with the game as the train rolls through the wilderness and into the interior. Outside the shortest day of the year has reduced daylight to only three hours, while the temperature is falling. In Fairbanks it will be minus 35°F.

F7 1522 pounds past Gold Creek with a southbound freight while No. 6 sits safely in the side track, May 25, 1975.

Extra 2501 north eases by a southbound freight and passenger train on May 27, 1975 in a narrow canyon. The Trans-Alaska pipeline construction boom is on; traffic is heavy carrying the pipe and vital materials to the construction site. Three-way meets such as this have become common on the single-track line.

Just empties goin' back. Caboose 1084 trails the string of empties, holding the main line, meeting No. 6 at a lonely siding in the interior. The traditional marker lamps have been replaced with reflective paddle boards. Ahead of the train it is all downhill on the run to Anchorage.

No. 5 takes the side track at Broad Pass in a rendezvous with its northbound counterpart on Sept. 4, 1977.

A southbound freight has cleared at Colorado, and fireman Louis Delberg and brakeman Jim Bruckman align the switch to allow No. 6 to come back on the main line and proceed north on Aug. 14, 1979.

The highest point on the railroad, at milepost 312.5, is also the lowest crossing of the divide in the Rocky Mountain chain and is within sight of the highest mountain (20,320 ft.) in North America, only 60 miles distant.

FP7 1530 has just cleared the Nenana Canyon with No. 5 at milepost 347. The train is still on the north slope of the Alaska range, making a steady climb to the summit some 30 miles ahead.

There are 36 Summits on railroad lines in North America. The one in Alaska is 2,363 feet above sea level as it crosses the continental divide 228 miles north of Anchorage. Summit Lake divides its waters, half going south to empty into the Cook Inlet arm of the Pacific and half to the Bering Sea by way of the Yukon River. This scene also shows the well-maintained roadbed.

Seven inches above the ground. Although not the most glamorous aspect of railroading, track work is of vital importance and much attention is given to maintenance. The maintenance-of-way department has the responsibility of keeping the track, bridges and buildings in good condition. The 115-pound rail gets new ties at Lagoon (now Oliver) while the gang works on the roadbed. **Courtesy: William F. Coghill, Alaska Railroad.**

Extra 3007 south is caught at milepost 346 near Denali Park station on May 27, 1978. Five big units easily handle the string of empties.

No. 5 meets No. 6 midway between Anchorage and Fairbanks. A few passengers traded trains here, as evidenced by the conductor ready to board. A Broad Pass turn (or wherever the trains meet) is a popular summer outing through the wilds.

Heading due north at Summit, No. 6, The AuRoRa, has reached the highest point on the line, 2,363 feet above sea level. Since early morning it has been climbing the long continuous grade that stretches back almost 150 miles from Matanuska.

General Manager Steve Ditmeyer and his wife, Marti, share a plate of cookies and pie from the business car with the engine crew at Denali Park station on August 15, 1979. Fireman Louis Delberg accepts the gift.

Mt. McKinley. A camera cannot do justice to the beauty of the great mountain. Tourists flock to this greatest attraction in Alaska. The huge land mass is accessible only by bus from Denali Park station. It is a rare day when the mountain is visible, or "out." The huge, icy throne makes its own weather and is usually cloud-covered. The name of the park, but not the mountain, has been changed. It is now called "Denali" Park from an Athabascan word meaning "The Great One."

GP 40 3003 eases past No. 6 making a stop at McKinley Park, now Denali Park station on Sept. 4, 1977. Labor day marks the end of the tourist season; service is reduced to twice-weekly round trips; the station is closed for the winter, and the freight trains roll through almost unnoticed. The AuRoRa and the Denali Express will carry more than 70,000 passengers in a year to and from the park.

The 1953-built EMD FP7 1510, not yet selected to commemorate the 200th anniversary of the nation, on Sept. 7, 1975, as it is welcomed at what is now Denali Park.

FP7 1510 in Bicentennial dress leads No. 6 across Riley Creek bridge at milepost 347 on a bright fall day in 1977. The trees are full, but soon the leaves will turn golden when winter closes in and the interior rests in quiet, white solitude.

Independence Day 1978 is celebrated at McKinley Park (now Denali) with the arrival of a red, white and blue 1512.

The Fairbanks passenger train slips under the framework of the massive highway bridge crossing the Nenana Canyon, bores through a wood-lined tunnel, and winds its way along the canyon into Healy.

No. 5 is one and a half hours late at McKinley Park station (now Denali Park) on July 4, 1978, because of heavy summer north-end passenger traffic. The passengers are in their places, the dome car is filled, the last of the baggage is worked, and the conductor checks his watch before giving the engineer the high sign to continue the journey to Anchorage.

President Warren G. Harding drove the golden spike into the rails at Nenana while on a goodwill tour to Alaska. It was a journey from which he did not return; he was taken ill and died in San Francisco Aug. 2, 1923.

A southbound freight hugs a shelf of a shifting mountain in the Nenana Canyon. Evidence of the continuous battle to shore up the roadbed is seen here. Centuries-old permafrost is melting, causing the mountain to shift, taking the track with it.

Few sights on a railroad are more dramatic than a train entering or emerging from a tunnel. No. 5 dramatizes this point as it darts into the north portal at Garner. Courtesy: William F. Coghill, Alaska Railroad.

The line traverses rugged mountain country on its journey into the deep interior. The Nenana Canyon provides the easiest access through the Alaska range, which divides the south central region from the interior.

Construction crews add yard tracks at Healy in 1978, because of an increase in coal traffic. Greater interest in Alaska coal may cause further expansions. Courtesy: William F. Coghill, Alaska Railroad.

On Aug. 30, 1980, No. 5 eases by the newly constructed yard and into Healy. The freight cars contain coal from the nearby mines, which will be shipped to Fairbanks.

A GP7 teams with a RSD4 to pull a coal train to Fairbanks and waits for a southbound freight to clear the main line at Healy on Oct. 27, 1977.

Healy awaits the arrival of a train on Aug. 15, 1979. The Alaska railroad's largest source of on-line revenue comes from the Usibelli coal mines, located in the canyon to the right of town.

Healy is a coal town, from which more than 8400 carloads are shipped to power plants. Some may be shipped to Pacific rim countries. No. 6 stops on May 27, 1978.

The river town of Nenana plays host to No. 5, the Fairbanks-Anchorage passenger train, on May 28, 1978. Nenana is the place where cargo is transferred to river boats which serve the small native fishing villages along the Tanana and Yukon rivers. The freight is stored all winter, and at first thaw, the barges and cargo move downriver.

Rick Whiteside grabs the iron and swings onto the rear unit of a southbound extra freight at Healy on May 27, 1978. The "railroad is his" for the 244-mile nonstop run to Anchorage. The five Geeps will easily handle the 100 or so empty cars, since most of the trip will be downhill.

A distant trackside view of the Nenana station taken in October 1977. The station is used for passengers and freight. Built in 1922, it is a frame structure consisting of a main block of two stories with a single story wing.

A few passengers greet the train on an August day in 1979. Nenana is famous for its Ice Classic in which a prize is given to the person who guesses the day and time the ice will break and begin to move down river. The collapse of a tripod, imbedded in the Tanana river ice, trips a wire and stops the clock, marking the traditional beginning of spring in interior Alaska.

The "Mears Memorial Bridge," one of the longest single span bridges in the world, crosses the Tanana river at Nenana. The long ascending 10 degree curve is shown in this dramatic view. Courtesy: William F. Coghill, Alaska Railroad.

A 701-foot single span steel bridge crosses the Tanana River at Nenana, milepost 411.7. A long 10 degree horseshoe curve permits an easy ascending approach to the bridge. The bridge stands high to clear river traffic. No. 5 crosses the bridge on May 28, 1978, 55 years after President Harding drove the golden spike completing the railroad.

No. 5 at the Fairbanks station on May 30, 1976 waits to load passengers for Denali Park, Anchorage and points in be-tween. Note the ''1776'' on the number board, displayed in celebration of the nation's 200th birthday.

A modern station, serving the interior city of Fairbanks, is the northernmost station on the North American conti-nent, 120 miles from the Arctic Circle. Located in the center of the city, on the banks of the Chena River, the station is close to the business center of Fairbanks, which makes it popular with tourists.

No. 5 waits at the south end of the Fairbanks yard on Sept. 2, 1980, to meet a Healy coal train, powered by a rebuilt low nose GP7. A fresh covering of snow on Labor Day weekend indicates that winter can, and does, come at any time in Fairbanks.

In an unusually early snow storm, the AuRoRa is ready to depart from the north end of the main line on Sept. 2, 1980.

Ken C. Brovald, author of "Alaska's Wilderness Rails, from the Taiga to the Tundra." Photo was taken at Portage, Alaska, on Jan. 6, 1979, while Brovald accompanied the Alaska Railroad superintendent over the line.

About the author:

Ken C. Brovald spent his "growing up" years along the Great Northern Railway. The exposure to a mainline railroad in action stimulated a lifelong interest in railroads and a fever to pursue the interest. He has now spent 20 years in this avocation and has written several articles on trains and railroads for such periodicals as Pacific News, Rail Classics, *and* Trains.

This book is his first full-length review of a major railroad, a subject which he found to be virtually untouched by on-the-scene photographer. He lives in Anchorage with his wife, Arlene, who shares his railroading interests.